The End of the Night

Ben Brown lives in London. His plays include *Four Letter Word* (Edinburgh Fringe; Cameron Mackintosh New Writing Award); *All Things Considered* (Stephen Joseph Theatre, Hampstead Theatre, Petit Théâtre de Paris, Marian Street Theatre, Sydney, Zimmertheater, Heidelberg); *Larkin With Women* (Stephen Joseph Theatre, West Yorkshire Playhouse, Coventry Belgrade, Manchester Library Theatre, Orange Tree Theatre; Express Play of the Year, TMA Best New Play); *The Promise* (Orange Tree Theatre); *Three Days in May* (national tour and West End; WhatsOnStage Best New Play, Mexican Critics Best New Play); and *A Splinter of Ice* (national tour and Jermyn Street Theatre, London).

T0322543

BEN BROWN

The End of the Night

faber

First published in 2022
by Faber and Faber Limited
74–77 Great Russell Street
London WC1B 3DA

Typeset by Brighton Gray
Printed and bound in the UK by CPI Group (Ltd), Croydon CR0 4YY

A CIP record for this book
is available from the British Library

978-0-571-37707-6

8 10 9 7

Introduction

I never thought I would write a play about the Holocaust until, a few years ago, I read a reference in a newspaper to Himmler having had a masseur who persuaded him to meet and negotiate with Jews.

So I got hold of Felix Kersten's memoirs and eventually found the story of the secret meeting he arranged between Himmler and Norbert Masur, a Swedish Jew, in his house north of Berlin on the night of 20 April 1945 – Hitler's last birthday.

Then I found Masur's account of the meeting, which he wrote for the Swedish section of the World Jewish Congress as soon as he got back to Stockholm. And the Nazis' Head of Foreign Intelligence, Walter Schellenberg, also wrote about the meeting.

Sarah Sigal and Richard Beecham organised a reading of the play at the JW3 in London in May 2019, after which the Park planned a production for the following September, delayed of course by Covid. But it seems fitting that the first performance is now taking place on the evening of 27 April – Yom HaShoah (Holocaust Remembrance Day).

Ben Brown,
March, 2022

For my uncle, Malcolm Brown

With thanks to Diarmid O'Sullivan, Jane Stapleton, Tom Littler and David Horovitch

The End of the Night premiered at Park Theatre, London, as a co-production with Original Theatre, on 27 April 2022, with the following cast and creative team:

Jeanne Bommezjin Olivia Bernstone
Norbert Masur Ben Caplan
Heinrich Himmler Richard Clothier
Felix Kersten Michael Lumsden
Elisabeth Lube Audrey Palmer

Director Alan Strachan
Set and Costume Designer Michael Pavelka
Lighting Designer Jason Taylor
Sound Designer Gregory Clarke
Assistant Director Tom Brain
Production Manager Tammy Rose

Producers Daniel Cooper & Tom Hackney
Production Co-ordinator Charlotte Holder
Company Stage Manager Lauren Barclay
Assistant Stage Manager Jeffrey Harmer
Stage Management Intern Alex Jaouen

PR Mobius
Artwork Designer Rebecca Pitt
Promotional Photography Michael Wharley
Rehearsal Photography Mark Douet
Videography Piers Foley

Artistic Director, Park Theatre Jez Bond
Executive Director, Park Theatre Vicky Hawkins
Artistic Director, Original Theatre Alastair Whatley

Characters

Norbert Masur

Felix Kersten

Elisabeth Lube

Heinrich Himmler

Jeanne Bommezjin

Setting

*The play takes place at Dr Felix Kersten's estate,
seventy kilometres north of Berlin between
19 and 21 April 1945.*

THE END OF THE NIGHT

'There is no greater duty than the redeeming of captives.'
Maimonides

SCENE ONE

The lights come up on a middle-aged man at the front of the stage.
This is Norbert Masur. He wears a suit and tie.

Masur Of course, it wasn't supposed to be me.

Beat.

It was supposed to be our chairman, Hillel Storch, the Swedish representative of the World Jewish Congress . . . He was the person who knew Dr Kersten and had agreed to meet his patient, Heinrich Himmler, in Berlin in the dying days of the war . . . But as a stateless ex-Latvian who'd already lost eighteen members of his family to the Nazis, Storch was eventually persuaded that it might be better if someone else went . . .

Beat.

So, after a brief battle with my conscience, and against the wishes of my wife . . . I volunteer . . . and as I was brought up in Germany but now have a Swedish passport, am chosen.

He looks concerned.

My mission, supported by a government keen to atone for its neutrality, is to try to persuade Himmler to stop the killing and torture of concentration camp prisoners and instead allow as many as possible to be rescued by the Red Cross and taken to Sweden . . . But why would Himmler, of all people, agree, when I have nothing to offer him in return? . . . Indeed, why has he even agreed to meet me? Kersten persuaded him apparently, but how? And why is

3

Kersten taking such a risk himself? He is, after all, only his masseur . . .

He looks puzzled.

Several agonising weeks later, and with a worsening war situation in Germany, on the morning of Thursday the 19th April, 1945, I at last hear news that Himmler is ready for us . . . So after a final briefing from the Swedish Foreign Office, Kersten and I board a plane marked with the swastika and take the noon postal service flight from Stockholm to Berlin . . . Seated amongst the Red Cross parcels, we are the only passengers.

Pause.

Now I have time to think about my mission . . . I've been involved in other help missions before, but always from the safety of Stockholm. This time it's action at the front lines, and for me, as a Jew, it's a deeply stirring thought that in a few hours I will meet the man primarily responsible for the destruction of several million of my people . . . and that the lives of thousands of others may depend on my words.

He reflects.

At around six o'clock, we arrive at Tempelhof airport and are greeted by a group of half a dozen men in suits and fedoras, who Kersten later confirms are the Gestapo. 'Heil Hitler,' they say. 'Good evening,' I reply, taking off my hat . . . Kersten shows them his entry visa, whilst I, not having one, keep my passport in my pocket . . . Kersten then shows them my safe conduct, which simply says that anyone in his company must be allowed through without further enquiry, since no one besides Himmler is to know of my visit . . . Fortunately, it works, and safely through border control we are driven away in a Gestapo car.

Beat.

After half an hour and several detours to avoid bombed-out streets, we are out of Berlin and on the highway, though driving without lights, our progress is slow. Next we reach the town of Oranienburg, where many of my relatives were interned before I was able to get them to Sweden . . . Finally, close to midnight, we turn off the main road, drive through a wood and arrive at our destination, an estate belonging to Kersten, where we are to wait for Himmler . . . Its name is Gut Hartzwalde.

> *A plump man, Dr Felix Kersten, joins Masur as they walk to the front door of Gut Hartzwalde, Kersten's estate seventy kilometres north of Berlin. Both carry overnight bags.*
> *Almost midnight on 19 April 1945.*
> *The sound of an occasional plane overhead. Far-off explosions and gunfire.*

Kersten Do you like it? I bought it with my blocked German earnings at the start of the war. But last year Himmler allowed me to move my family to Sweden, as long as I promised to come back and treat him every fourth month . . . The farm is run by some Jehovah's Witnesses I persuaded Himmler to let me relocate from Buchenwald.

> *Something is stopping Kersten from opening the front door.*

Oh, it's bolted from the inside. I shall have to ring the bell and wake Elisabeth.

Masur Elisabeth?

Kersten My housekeeper. She looks after everything when I'm away.

> *He rings the bell.*

Elisabeth!

A light appears in the hall and a woman in her sixties enters in her dressing gown carrying a candle.

Elisabeth Is that you, Felix?

Kersten Yes, of course.

Elisabeth Oh, thank God.

Kersten But I can't get in.

Elisabeth Sorry, I've bolted it. You never know who might be out there.

Kersten No, but can you unbolt it now, please?

She does so and the door opens.

Thank you.

Kersten and Elisabeth look at each other with affection. Then embrace.

Elisabeth Thank God, you're here. I've been terrified you'd been killed on the way by one of those terrible aeroplanes. There are so many now. Shooting and bombing all the time.

Kersten My dear Elisabeth, you mustn't worry about me. You know I'm indestructible.

Elisabeth Don't say that, you'll tempt fate. Now come in quick before they see the light. Not that we have much, now the electricity has gone.

They go inside.

Kersten This is Mr Masur, who I've brought from Sweden.

Elisabeth Yes, of course . . . Welcome to Hartzwalde, Mr Masur.

Masur Thank you.

Kersten Elisabeth and I have been friends for twenty years.

Elisabeth Twenty-*three* years . . .

6

Kersten I was her lodger.

Elisabeth My parents' lodger, God bless their souls . . . But as soon as you arrived in Berlin, it was clear someone had to look after you. Before you married Irmgard, that is.

Kersten Yes . . . Anyway, it is good to be back in what I like to call my little Finnish island in the woods. My sanctuary. But you will see how beautiful it is in the morning . . . Now, Elisabeth, I have brought some goodies with me. Tea, coffee, sugar and pastries from Stockholm.

He takes a brown paper bag out of his larger bag.

Elisabeth Wonderful. (*To Masur.*) He always does, you know, which is just as well as it's impossible to buy anything here. I shall put them in the larder immediately.

He gives her the bag.

But you must be starving. Would you like to eat some now?

Kersten No. We must save them all for the Reichsführer tomorrow. So perhaps just a bowl of soup and some bread. And some cheese. And some cold meat perhaps . . . We have a big day tomorrow, don't we, Masur?

Masur (*with concern*) Yes, we do . . .

Elisabeth Of course . . . And you will want to go to bed after that, so I will get it as soon as I can.

Kersten Thank you, Elisabeth.

Masur Thank you.

She goes.

Kersten Ah, no one looks after me like she does . . .

Beat.

Now, I think we deserve a drink, don't you?

Masur Well . . . I could do with one.

Kersten leads the way to the parlour.

Kersten What would you like? I warn you, I only have wine now. And not much of that. But I guess we might as well finish it up . . . Red or white?

Masur Red, please.

They go into the parlour, which has a table and chairs and a divan to the side. And in the corner, a gramophone and some records.
Masur follows him.

Kersten Wait a minute. I just need to pull the curtains. So the Russians don't see us. Or the Gestapo.

He smiles.
Masur doesn't.
Kersten goes over to the windows and pulls the curtains closed.
The room is plunged into darkness for a moment.
Then a match is struck as Kersten lights candles.

That's better. Now, please, sit down. Make yourself at home.

Masur Thank you . . . though I could hardly feel less at home.

Kersten . . . Why do you say that?

Masur Because I must be the only free Jew in Germany right now.

Kersten Ah . . .

He considers this.

Yes, I should think you probably are, actually . . . Though there must be some hiding in cellars, and attics, and haylofts and so forth. But they're hardly free, are they? And others still passing as Germans.

He uncorks the wine.

8

Anyway . . .

He pours two glasses and gives one to Masur.

Cheers.

Masur . . . Cheers.

They drink.

Kersten In actual fact, you are not in Germany now, so you needn't worry about the Gestapo paying us a visit.

Masur . . . I'm sorry?

Kersten Hartzwalde has been granted extra-territorial status, so technically it is not in Germany and the Gestapo can't come here without an invitation.

Masur How did you get that?

Kersten smiles.

Kersten I asked Himmler . . . At first he refused. He said Ribbentrop wouldn't allow it. But then one day I had an idea . . . I took a magnificent fresh ham to Berlin with me in my briefcase. And after I'd massaged Himmler and brought him to a state of blissful relaxation and well-being, I brought the ham out and asked him if he'd like a slice. Ravenous as he always is after his treatment, he cut a slice with his SS dagger, took a large bite and began chewing. 'Mm,' he said, 'this is good enough to eat on its own. Tender, savoury and just a little salty.' He took another mouthful before asking me how I managed to save up enough ration coupons to buy it. 'Oh, I didn't,' I replied. 'It's from Hartzwalde,' whereupon, of course, he started to splutter and choke and spat out the remainder of his mouthful into his hand. 'But this is terrible,' he said. 'Slaughtering livestock is a hanging offence in Germany.' 'Yes,' I said, 'and so is benefiting from it. You'd better grant Hartzwalde extra-territorial status.' And two days later I got a document signed by him and Ribbentrop confirming it.

He chuckles at the memory.

And ever since then we've eaten our ham without fear of discovery . . .

He remembers Masur is Jewish.

And other livestock . . . And the Gestapo can't bump me off as they would like to.

Masur Why would they like to?

Kersten Because of my influence over Himmler. They're jealous. But they're not allowed here so I'm all right . . . though they once tried to get round that by assassinating me on my way to Berlin.

Masur reacts.

Masur You're joking?

Kersten No. Himmler found out and told me to take another route just in time, so I had a lucky escape. And now he's told Kaltenbrunner that he holds him personally responsible for my safety and that if I die he dies, so I should be all right.

Elisabeth enters with the soup.

Elisabeth Now, this should warm you up.

Kersten Ah, good. Elisabeth is famous for her soups.

Elisabeth Well, I hope you like it. It's chicken and vegetable.

Kersten With mushrooms from the woods, I trust.

Elisabeth Of course.

Kersten Excellent.

Masur It sounds delicious.

Kersten Please, tuck in.

They eat.

Masur Mm, it is delicious.

Elisabeth Good . . . It is not so easy to produce good food these days, but I do what I can.

Masur Thank you.

Kersten You're a genius, Elisabeth.

Elisabeth Don't be silly.

Kersten You always say that, but it's true.

He smiles at Masur, who smiles back briefly before taking another mouthful.
Elisabeth goes.

Now, about tomorrow, when you meet the Reichsführer . . .

Masur Yes?

Kersten Well, I hope you don't mind me giving you some advice . . .

Masur Not at all. I'd welcome it.

Kersten Well then . . . try not to get into an argument with him.

Masur . . . How do you mean?

Kersten I mean about the past . . . about what's been happening, to your people . . . What's done is done and cannot be undone.

Masur True . . .

Kersten So humour him.

Masur . . . Humour him?

Kersten Yes, be patient. Tolerant, if not forgiving. Or pretend to be. Then he'll be more likely to give us what we want.

Masur considers this.

Masur I'll do my best.

Kersten Good.

They eat.

Masur What's he like?

Kersten Himmler . . .?

Masur Yes.

Kersten thinks.

Kersten Affable.

Masur . . . Affable?

Kersten Yes, he has a sense of humour. Not like Hitler, though I don't know Hitler. Himmler wanted me to treat him once but I managed to get out of it.

Masur How?

Kersten I said that his problem was mental and needed psychiatric expertise whereas my therapy was purely manual.

Masur Very wise.

Kersten Yes. He's just executed one of his doctors for letting his wife be captured by the Americans.

He drinks.

And he likes to be in control, of course. Himmler, I mean. It's said that when he was a young man he didn't approve of the woman his older brother was going to marry – he didn't think she was pure enough – and so hired a private investigator to find some dirt on her – or rather, evidence she wasn't a virgin – and presented it to his brother, who broke off the engagement . . . And now all the men in the SS have to present potential wives to him for his approval and he studies pictures of them for Aryan qualities.

He sips his soup.

Masur What does he want from me then? I don't have any Aryan qualities, and he must have plenty on his plate already.

Kersten Yes . . .

Masur So why is he seeing me?

Kersten thinks.

Kersten He wants, I believe, to make peace with you.

Masur Peace?

Kersten Yes, as a representative of the Jews.

Masur takes this in.

Masur . . . Isn't it a little late for that?

Kersten Possibly. But as there are still so many lives at stake, you might want to hear him out . . .

Masur And that's all he wants?

Kersten I believe so. He said it's time to bury the hatchet.

Masur . . . He said that?

Kersten Yes. But I think it's best to let him speak for himself. So . . .

He gets up.

Let me show you to your room so you can get a good night's sleep before you meet him tomorrow.

Masur Thank you.

Masur gets up too.

Tell me just one more thing though.

Kersten Yes?

Masur Why are you doing this?

Kersten How do you mean?

Masur Why are you going to all this trouble and taking such a risk when you could have stayed in Sweden?

Kersten hesitates.

Kersten Because I can. Who else could introduce you to Himmler and perhaps save thousands of lives?

Masur takes this in.

And incidentally, we are not the only ones taking a risk. Do you know what the Reichsführer said when I first suggested this meeting? 'But I could never receive a Jew. The Führer would have me shot on the spot.'

He smiles.

Masur What changed his mind?

Kersten I pointed out that as he was in charge of the customs police, the Führer needn't know.

As they go out to the hall, Elisabeth enters with a tray and begins clearing the table.

(*Indicating.*) You're the second door on the left. The bathroom's at the end.

Masur Thank you.

Kersten . . . Goodnight.

Masur Goodnight.

Masur goes.
    Kersten comes back into the parlour as Elisabeth finishes loading the tray.

Elisabeth Felix, I'm frightened.

Kersten Why?

Elisabeth Because the Russians are coming. They are already at the Oder. It's said they will be here within days. Oh, Felix, they will kill you and rape me. Whole gangs of them. That's what they've been doing, you know. They are without mercy. They will not spare us as 'extra-territorial'.

Kersten None of that is going to happen. We're going to Sweden on Saturday.

Elisabeth It's all right for you, you're Finnish. But how can I? I'm a German.

Kersten Yes, and so is Irmgard, and the children. So the Reichsführer will give you safe conduct, as he has Masur. And then you will be safe and free forever with us in Stockholm.

Elisabeth Then why can't we go now, tonight?

Kersten Tonight? There is no plane tonight.

Elisabeth Tomorrow morning then?

Kersten Because there is something we must do first.

Elisabeth What?

Kersten Persuade the Reichsführer to release some prisoners. Then he will give you safe conduct and the Swedish government will allow us to stay when we get there. And allow me to practise physiotherapy. I've made a deal with them, you see. Livelihood for lives.

Elisabeth is still worried.

So trust me. Have I ever let you down?

Elisabeth No . . .

Kersten Well then. We're survivors, aren't we?

She nods.
He smiles and puts his arm round her shoulders.

Come now, get yourself to bed. We must get some sleep.

She nods and takes the tray out.
He goes too as the lights fade to black.

SCENE TWO

20 April, 9 a.m.
The sound of distant planes.
Then the lights come up on Kersten at the breakfast table.
He is eating as Masur enters.

Kersten Ah, good morning. Come and have some breakfast.

Masur Thank you.

Masur sits down and helps himself.

Kersten Coffee?

Masur Please.

Kersten pours him some.

Kersten How did you sleep?

Masur Well . . . I got some.

Kersten I know, it's not easy with the noise of the planes, is it?

Masur No.

He eats tentatively.

What time will the Reichsführer be arriving?

Kersten Ah, yes . . . now I'm afraid there's been a delay. His adjutant telephoned to say he won't arrive until late tonight.

Masur (*disappointed*) Oh . . .

Kersten You see, today is a special day.

16

Masur Is it?

Kersten Yes. The Führer's birthday. April 20th. So, of course, the Reichsführer must attend his birthday party.

Masur Oh . . .

Kersten Not that I can believe it will be a very happy occasion this year, being held as it is in a bunker.

Masur No . . . But I hope the Reichsführer will come here straight afterwards. I'm keen to get back to Sweden as soon as possible.

Kersten Yes, so am I . . . But don't worry. He'll come tonight, I'm sure.

Masur Good.

Masur thinks.

But if his adjutant telephoned, then he knows I'm here too?

Kersten Yes. But you needn't worry about Brandt. He's completely loyal to Himmler.

Masur . . . And no one else knows?

Kersten No.

Masur Apart from Elisabeth.

Kersten Well, of course. But you don't have to worry about her.

The sound of explosions nearby.
Masur is startled.

It's all right, they're not aiming at us but at the railway track a couple of kilometres away. So they're very unlikely to hit us.

He smiles.
Masur is hardly reassured.

Masur How much longer do you think the war will last?

Kersten A matter of weeks at most. If not days. So it's lucky we didn't come any later.

Beat.

Masur But I still don't know what he wants from me . . . Last year, when he let those Jewish prisoners from Theresienstadt go to Switzerland, he demanded money, didn't he?

Kersten So I gather. Five million Swiss francs . . . raised in America apparently.

Masur I can't do that. I have no authority for it.

Kersten Of course not. There's no question of that.

Masur Then what does he want? Besides 'peace with the Jews' . . .

Kersten hesitates.

Kersten Let's see what he says when he gets here.

He puts his napkin on the table.

Now, if you've finished, I'll give you a tour round the estate. We have a long wait till the Reichsführer comes.

Masur Thank you, I should like that.

Kersten Good.

They get up.

And this evening we can listen to Dr Goebbels' birthday broadcast on the radio, if you feel inclined.

Masur Oh yes . . . I wouldn't want to miss that . . .

Kersten smiles and they go off as the lights fade.

Evening.
In the darkness we hear the voice of Goebbels on the
radio.

Goebbels (*on radio*) German citizens . . . at the moment of
the war when – so it seems – all forces of hate and
destruction have been gathered once again, perhaps for the
final time, in the west, the east, the southeast, and the south,
seeking to break through our front and give the death blow
to the Reich, I once again speak to the German people on
the 20th of April about the Führer, just as I have every year
since 1933. That has happened at good and bad times in the
past. But never before did things stand on such a knife edge,
never before did the German people have to defend their
very lives under such enormous danger, never before did the
Reich have to draw on its last strength to protect its very
existence.

> *During the above, the lights have gradually come up on*
> *the parlour bathed in candlelight with the curtains*
> *closed.*
>   *Kersten and Masur hold glasses of red wine as they sit*
> *and listen.*

Now this is not the time to speak of the Führer's birthday
in the usual way or to present him with the usual best
wishes.

Kersten I should say.

Goebbels More must be said this evening and by one who
has won the right both from the Führer and the people.
I have been at the Führer's side for more than twenty years.
I have seen his rise and that of his movement from the
smallest and most improbable beginnings up to the great
seizure of power. I have shared joy and sorrow with the
Führer, from unprecedented historic victories to terrible

setbacks in the remarkable years from 1939 until now. I stand beside him tonight as fate challenges him and his people with its last, most severe test. I am confident that fate will give him the laurel wreath of victory.

Kersten snorts and Masur smiles faintly as they exchange a look.

Once more the armies of the enemy powers storm against our defensive fronts. Behind them is the slavering force of International Jewry that wants no peace until it has reached its satanic goal of world destruction. But its hopes are in vain. As he has done so often before, God will throw Lucifer back into the abyss even as he stands before the gates of power over all the peoples. A man of truly timeless greatness, of unique courage, of a steadfastness that elevates the hearts of some and shakes those of others, will be his tool. Who will claim that this man can be found in the leadership of Bolshevism or plutocracy? No, the German people bore him. It chose him. By free election it made him Führer. It knows his works of peace and now wants to bear and fight the war that was forced upon him until its successful end.

Kersten Good luck with that.

Goebbels So now we stand behind him with fortitude and courage. Soldier and civilian, man, woman and child – a people determined to do all to defend its life and honour . . . He may look his enemies in the eye, for we promise him that he does not need to look behind him. We will not waver or weaken. We will never desert him, no matter how desperate and dangerous the hour. We stand with him, as he stands with us – in Germanic loyalty as we have sworn, as we shall fulfil . . . Never will history record that in these days a people deserted its Führer or a Führer deserted his people. And that is victory.

Kersten Ah . . .

Goebbels We have often wished the Führer in happy times our best on this evening. Today in the midst of suffering and danger, our greeting is much deeper and more profound. May he remain what he is to us and always was – Our Hitler!

There is a burst of applause.
    Kersten gets up and turns the radio off.
    Silence.
    Then the telephone rings.
    They look at each other for a moment.
    Kersten answers it.

Kersten Hello? . . . Yes . . . Very well . . . Goodbye.

He replaces the receiver.

That was his adjutant. He'll be here by one.

Masur takes this in.
    He looks exhausted already.
    Kersten sits back down as the lights fade slowly to black.

SCENE FOUR

The same.
    In the darkness the sound of planes and far-off bombing.
    Gradually the lights fade up again on the candlelit scene.
    It's 2.30 a.m.
    Kersten is fast asleep and snoring.
    Masur dozes fitfully.
    The sound of a car pulling up outside the house.
    Masur wakes.

Masur Dr Kersten.

Kersten continues to snore.

Dr Kersten!

Kersten finally wakes up.

Kersten What?

Masur I think he's here.

Kersten Ah . . . good.

Kersten gets up and goes to the window.
He looks behind the curtain as the engine is turned off.

Yes, that's Brandt opening the door for him now. You stay here and I will bring him in to you.

Masur nods as Kersten goes out of the room.
Car doors slam shut.
Masur stays and waits nervously.
We hear voices in the hall.

(*Off.*) Herr Reichsführer, so good to see you.

Himmler (*off*) My dear Kersten, sorry I'm so late. I've come straight from the Führer's birthday celebration. And the roads now are not without their challenges . . .

Kersten (*off*) Yes, of course . . . Please leave your coat and cap here and then come through.

Himmler (*off*) Thank you.

Himmler enters, followed by Kersten.
Himmler, forty-four, is dressed impeccably in a grey military uniform (with the insignia of rank and shiny decorations), boots and round steel-rimmed spectacles. He wears a Totenkopf (death's head, or skull and cross bones) ring on his finger and a gun in a holster on his right hip, held up by his belt.
Himmler and Masur face each other.
Beat.

Kersten Reichsführer, allow me to introduce Mr Masur . . . of the World Jewish Congress.

Himmler . . . Good evening, Mr Masur.

Masur Good evening.

They shake hands.

Himmler Or perhaps we should say morning, as it's now past two.

Kersten Yes.

Kersten laughs and looks at Masur, but he merely gives the flicker of a smile.

Himmler In any case, welcome to Germany.

Masur Thank you.

Himmler I'm only sorry you had to come in such difficult circumstances. Is it your first time here?

Masur No, actually. I was brought up here.

Himmler (*surprised*) Oh . . . whereabouts?

Masur Friedrichstadt, near the Danish border. But I left over twenty years ago now.

Himmler Ah . . . And do you have any family still here?

Masur No . . . Not any more.

A charged moment.
Kersten steps in.

Kersten Now, though, before we sit down, may I offer you both some coffee?

Himmler Yes, please.

Masur Thank you.

Kersten Good. I shall go and ask Elisabeth to make some then.

Elisabeth enters with coffee, pastries and plates on a tray.

Elisabeth No need. I already have it all prepared.

Kersten Of course you do.

Himmler You are a marvel, Miss Lube. I don't know what Dr Kersten would do without you.

She smiles uncertainly.

Elisabeth Thank you, Herr Reichsführer. But Dr Kersten brought the pastries himself from Sweden.

Himmler Ah, how thoughtful.

She puts the tray on the table.

Elisabeth Please, gentlemen. Help yourselves.

She goes.
They hesitate until Himmler waves Masur to go first.

Himmler After you.

Masur Thank you.

They get themselves coffee.
Then Himmler picks up the milk jug and looks into it.

Himmler Fresh milk?

Kersten The advantages of living on a farm. And we are extra-territorial here, remember?

Himmler Of course . . . then I suppose it's all right.

He pours some milk into his coffee.
Kersten smiles.

Kersten Have a pastry.

Himmler does so and takes a bite.

Himmler Mm . . . Delicious. You must enjoy living in Sweden, Dr Kersten.

Kersten Yes . . . though of course I miss Germany, or Germany as it was before the war at least.

Himmler Yes . . .

Himmler reflects darkly as he drinks his coffee.

Now, let us get down to business, shall we? Time is short.

Kersten Of course.

He puts on a more serious face.

Himmler Mr Masur, as you have been out of this country for some years, perhaps you will allow me to tell you about the relations between our two peoples since you left?

Masur . . . Please do.

Himmler Thank you.

He thinks.

You see, my generation have never known peace. When the First World War began, I was fourteen years old . . . Four years later, after all the fighting and sacrifice, we lost the war because we were stabbed in the back by the Jewish-influenced government while our best men were at the front. So it turned out two million had died in vain . . .

Masur glances at Kersten but says nothing.

Then there was the civil war in which Jews like Rosa Luxemburg were deeply involved. And in 1919, when I was nineteen, the Bolsheviks took over my home town of Munich and declared it a Soviet Republic! So you can hardly blame us for supporting the man who proclaimed his aim as the destruction of Bolshevism, and was prepared to go to prison to achieve it.

Masur But very few Jews were Bolsheviks.

Himmler Many of their leaders in Germany seemed to be. And of course it was a Jew, Marx, who invented the whole communist idea . . . But in any case, the Jews were an alien element here which always evoked irritation. So after we came to power, we were determined to solve the problem once and for all . . . Now, as it happens, I was always in favour of a humane solution through emigration. But no other countries would take your people. Even in the West, which claims to be so hospitable to Jews, only a fraction of the number wanting to go there were taken in, as the world saw when that ship with nine hundred was turned away from the shores of America just before the war. And meanwhile the English demanded that every Jew should take at least a thousand pounds out of the country with him, so only the rich Jews could go there, before they took in a few thousand children, but not their parents, of course . . . Then, after the war began, I hoped we could send them all – you all – to Madagascar, which France could give us in recompense for its animosity. But Britain's continued hostility made it impossible as its navy would have prevented it. So you see, internment was our only option. But I am delighted that emigration is now back on the table as that has always been my preferred solution.

Masur glances at Kersten.

Masur . . . I can see that it might have been more comfortable for the German people not to have a minority in its midst. But it has never been in accordance with international law, or morality, to drive people from a country in which they and their ancestors have lived for generations . . . Of course, out of necessity, the Jews tried to emigrate. But the National Socialists wanted a situation, which had been created over several centuries, to be changed within a few years, and that was impossible.

Himmler Impossible? We did not find it so . . . But in any case, in revenge for our determination to clear the Jews out of Germany, your people started a war against us in 1939.

Masur . . . We started the war?

Himmler Yes, egged on by the Jewish press, Britain and France declared war.

Masur But that was because, after you'd already annexed Austria and Czechoslovakia, they didn't want you to take over any more of Europe. As ever, they wanted to stop any European country getting too powerful. It was nothing to do with the Jews.

Himmler smiles.

Himmler Well, either way, the Jews became our opponents – a fifth column in our own land – so naturally we could not allow them to remain free then. You must see that?

Kersten steps in.

Kersten It seems to me that we are discussing which came first, the chicken or the egg? But should we not move on to the present?

Himmler Almost. But given the appalling press we are now getting in Sweden, it is important that I explain to Mr Masur how we reached this state of affairs.

He thinks.

Because then, in the summer of 1941, the war brought us into contact with the Jewish masses in the East, which changed everything, because we could not tolerate such an enemy at our backs. And you cannot deny that the Jews were our enemies and wished us ill.

Masur How could they not when you'd treated them the way you had?

Himmler That's as may be . . . But you must understand that the war in the East was unbelievably difficult. A terrible climate, never-ending distances, an enemy population, and constantly appearing partisans. We had to conquer or perish, as the Führer said. And only by being harsh could the troops prevail. So they were forced to destroy whole villages if there was resistance and shooting from them. And these Eastern Jews helped the partisans.

Masur How could they when you'd concentrated them in ghettoes?

Himmler They conveyed intelligence and fired on us from their ghettoes. And they are the carriers of diseases such as typhus. I lost thousands of my SS troops that way. So in order to control these epidemics, we had to cremate the bodies of the many people who died of these diseases, and that was the reason we built the crematoria. And now, because of this, everybody wants to tighten the noose around our neck.

Masur . . . That's why you built the crematoria?

Himmler Yes.

Masur restrains himself.

Masur And the concentration camps?

Himmler The bad reputation of these camps is because of the unfortunate choice of name for them. That was a mistake. We should have called them 'education camps'.

Masur Yes, well, I think we've had enough education now . . .

Beat.

And surely you don't deny that atrocities have occurred in the camps?

Himmler I concede that it has happened, occasionally. But I have also punished those responsible. Like the commandant of the Buchenwald camp, for example, whom I had shot for corruption and ill-treatment of prisoners just three weeks ago.

Masur Our information is that in the East many thousands have been murdered by shooting, injection, and some kind of gas.

Himmler (*quickly*) That is not true.

Masur . . . Isn't it?

Himmler No, of course not.

They look at each other.

Kersten Look, we don't want to discuss the past. We can't alter that. We need to discuss what and who can still be saved.

Himmler Very well, let us move on.

Masur Yes, let's.

Beat.

How many people are in the camps still under your control?

Himmler I don't have the precise figures, but taking Sachsenhausen, Theresienstadt, Mauthausen and Ravensbrück together, about a hundred thousand, I should think.

Masur . . . Is that all?

Himmler Yes. Most are now in the hands of the Allies. Including one hundred and fifty thousand in Auschwitz, I believe.

Masur Really? I'm told the number is more like six thousand, who were too ill for you to 'evacuate' to Germany.

Himmler Russian lies . . .

Beat.

Masur In any case, I'm sure you understand that all those still in your hands must be assured of their lives if we are to build a bridge between our peoples for the future.

Himmler Of course. And we are looking after them as well as we can, in the circumstances. But it is not easy, with our enemies at the gates.

Masur So why not release them? Then you won't have to look after them any more.

Himmler hesitates.

Himmler In actual fact, it was always my intention to turn over the concentration camps without defending them, as I told Kersten some time ago.

Kersten Yes . . .

Himmler So a couple of weeks ago I turned over Buchenwald to the Americans without a struggle, but what happened? They took pictures of some inmates who'd been burnt in a fire of their own making and blamed it on us . . . And the same thing happened at Bergen-Belsen just a few days ago when I turned it over to the British. They tied up a guard and photographed him with some prisoners who had just died of typhus and the pictures were then published all over the world as evidence of a systematic programme of extermination . . . So I can't win.

Masur So hand them over to a neutral country like Sweden?

Himmler Yes, I tried that too. A few months ago I let two thousand seven hundred Jews go from Theresienstadt to Switzerland but even that resulted in a press campaign against me. It was said that I only did it in order to establish an alibi for myself. *But I do not need an alibi.* I have always done what I believed to be right and necessary for my people and I will stand by that.

Masur I believe only twelve hundred in fact reached Switzerland.

Himmler Yes . . . It got into the press so we had to put a stop to it. But the point is I got no credit for it.

Masur glances at Kersten.

Masur On the contrary, I remember it going down very well in Sweden, especially as the people were in relatively good health.

Himmler Yes, well, Theresienstadt is a special case. Not so much a camp as a town run by and for Jews. Heydrich and I set it up before the war and hoped that one day all camps would be like that.

Masur Yes, well, I trust you won't be needing camps of any type now.

Himmler No . . . But the point is, nobody has been covered with dirt in the newspapers as I have these last twelve years. And the publication of atrocities as an incitement against me does not encourage me to continue my policy of turning over the camps without resistance. That is why, a few days ago, when the American tank columns closed in on a camp in Saxony, I had it evacuated. Why should I do anything else?

Masur Because it's the right and humane thing to do . . . whatever the newspapers make of it, which in a democracy is up to them.

Himmler Yes, but who runs the newspapers?

He looks at Masur pointedly.

Kersten Let's get down to specifics, shall we? What about handing over Ravensbrück to the Red Cross? Since it's just thirty kilometres from here, you could almost call it our local camp.

He smiles.

Masur Yes, that would be a good place to start.

Himmler considers this.

Himmler And if I were to, what is to stop the Swedish papers announcing in big headlines that the war criminal Himmler, in terror of punishment for his crimes, is trying to buy his freedom? Save his own skin . . . Nothing, according to Mr Masur.

Kersten The Swedish papers will know nothing about it, will they, Masur?

Masur Not from me.

Kersten And the Swedish government have guaranteed confidentiality too.

Himmler thinks.

Himmler But what about the transport? We can't spare any.

Masur The Swedes will provide the transport.

Kersten Yes. And to be frank, Herr Reichsführer, couldn't you do with the extra space in the camps for your own refugees now?

Himmler hesitates.

Himmler Mr Masur, would you mind if I discussed the matter with Dr Kersten in private for a moment?

Masur Not at all. I will wait outside.

Himmler Thank you.

Masur goes out.

Dr Kersten, there are over twenty thousand prisoners in Ravensbrück, now the male prisoners from the East have joined the women there.

Kersten Good. A sizeable number then.

Himmler Yes, but far too many to release. The Führer would be bound to find out.

Kersten Not necessarily, Herr Reichsführer. The situation has gone beyond that now, surely? And with the Führer stuck in Berlin . . .

Himmler thinks for a moment.

Himmler No, it is impossible . . . the whole thing is impossible.

He turns away in apparent physical pain.
Then rubs his stomach.

Kersten Are you all right, Herr Reichsführer?

Himmler No, my stomach is playing up . . . And no wonder. What was I thinking? Agreeing to meet a Jew . . . I should never have come here. I should have got some sleep instead.

He sits down wearily and in obvious pain.
Kersten looks at him.

Kersten May I make a suggestion, Herr Reichsführer?

Himmler stops.

Himmler What?

Kersten If you are in discomfort, why not let me relieve it?

Himmler is surprised.

Himmler Now?

Kersten Why not?

Himmler Well . . . I have a meeting in Hohenlychen at six.

Kersten But it's only three. And Mr Masur won't mind waiting, I'm sure. He wouldn't want you to be in pain.

Himmler considers it.

Himmler Very well . . . thank you . . . I could do with some relief . . .

He sits down again.
Kersten smiles at Himmler.

Kersten Good . . . You know what to do then.

Himmler Yes.

Himmler gets up and starts taking off his belt and gun.
He puts them on a chair.
Kersten goes to the gramophone and begins looking through the records.

This is very good of you, Dr Kersten. I didn't expect you to give me treatment in the middle of the night.

Kersten Anything to help, Herr Reichsführer.

Himmler continues to undress as Kersten chooses a record, takes it out of its sleeve and puts it on the gramophone.
Schubert's 'Ave Maria' begins.
Himmler stops for a moment as he hears the music.
Then continues getting undressed as Kersten takes off his jacket and begins rolling up his sleeves . . .
The lights cross-fade to Masur waiting outside the door. He looks puzzled as he hears the music.
Then continues waiting anxiously as the lights and music fade out.

SCENE FIVE

Another Schubert song ('An die Musik') plays in the darkness.
Then the lights fade up on the parlour, still bathed in candlelight.
Kersten gently massages Himmler's stomach as he lies on his back on the massage table in his socks and trousers with his eyes shut.
The song ends and the record finishes.
Kersten continues to massage him.

Himmler (*still with his eyes shut*) . . . I saw a deer on the way here, you know . . . hiding in the woods . . . Do you still like to hunt them?

Kersten Yes. When I have the time.

Himmler I don't understand it . . . How can you find pleasure in shooting at such poor innocent creatures? Properly considered, it's pure murder.

34

Kersten But don't you too?

Himmler reacts and opens his eyes.

Himmler What?

Kersten I mean, you used to go hunting, didn't you?

Himmler Oh, yes . . . but only to keep the numbers down. Never for pleasure.

Kersten Ah . . .

Himmler closes his eyes again.
Pause.

How is your family?

Himmler . . . Which one?

Kersten Both.

Himmler Gudrun is well, I believe. And growing up fast. She'll be sixteen in August . . . I haven't seen her for a while but she often writes . . . Margarete is still rather cold to me though.

Kersten Hardly surprising, I suppose . . .

Beat.

Himmler You do realise it was my duty to have more children than the one girl she was able to bear me?

Kersten Of course . . . How is your secretary?

Himmler Hedwig is no longer my secretary. And is now safely, I hope, in Berchtesgaden with the two little ones. Or relatively safely . . . I wish I were too . . .

Kersten . . . So why not imagine it for a moment.

Himmler What?

Kersten Imagine you are a boy again in Bavaria. Walking in the mountains. In your lederhosen.

Himmler thinks himself back.

Himmler Yes, those were the days . . . There is nowhere more beautiful than Bavaria . . . If only I could get back there . . .

Kersten . . . perhaps you can . . .

Himmler smiles at the thought.
Kersten continues massaging.

Himmler You know, Kersten, I sometimes think you are the only person I can really talk to. Talk freely to, I mean. The only person I can truly relax with.

Kersten I'm glad, Reichsführer. It is my job to relax you.

Himmler Well, I think you have now.

Kersten Good. Then I'll stop and just let you lie here for a moment.

Himmler Thank you . . .

Kersten gets up, takes a pastry and sits down at the table to eat it.
Himmler continues to lie back on the massage table.

Yes, I think you and Brandt are the only people I really trust.

Beat.

Kersten What about the Führer?

Himmler Well, of course. That goes without saying . . . Why do you even ask?

Kersten Oh . . . just because of the way he's treated you recently.

Himmler How do you mean?

Kersten hesitates.

Kersten Well, I don't like to say . . .

Himmler It's all right. You may speak freely.

Kersten Very well.

Beat.

Sacking you as Commander of Army Group Vistula – even as you were laid up with flu at Hohenlychen – as if anyone else could have stopped the Russians taking Pomerania . . . Taking the development of the secret weapons away from you, as if you were to blame for their imperfections . . . Insulting the SS by stripping the Leibstandarte Adolf Hitler of their armbands, as if they had any choice but to retreat from Hungary. Is it true that the men were so outraged they sent one of the armbands back to him with the arm of the fallen comrade still attached?

Himmler Yes . . .

He grimaces at the image.
  Kersten shakes his head.

Kersten It doesn't seem fair . . .

Himmler No . . .

Beat.

Kersten But it's none of my business, I suppose . . .

Himmler thinks.
  Kersten watches him.
  Pause.

How was the birthday dinner by the way?

Himmler flinches.

Himmler Indescribable . . .

He thinks back.

It began with news that Nuremberg had fallen and ended with the opening attack on Berlin, which we could hear from the Bunker.

Beat.

37

And yet he still refuses to leave for the Alpine Redoubt, though the last route through could be cut off at any moment . . . He simply said, 'How can I call on my troops to undertake this decisive battle for Berlin if at the same moment I myself withdraw to safety?' There seemed nothing more to say . . . Goering went south, as did Speer. Dönitz and I came north, and Goebbels and Bormann said they intend to stay with the Führer. So we all knew we might never see each other again . . . That's why I postponed this meeting till now. I didn't want to have to look the Führer in the face after meeting a Jew. I somehow felt he would know . . . assuming he doesn't already.

Kersten Oh no, I'm sure he doesn't.

Himmler No . . . but he was curt to me when I greeted him. He gave me a limp, indifferent handshake instead of his usual firm one.

Kersten Perhaps that's his Parkinson's disease?

Himmler No, that only affects his left arm. And he was noticeably warmer to some of the others . . . But then Bormann and Kaltenbrunner are poisoning him against me, I'm sure. And he is too weak to resist them.

Kersten hesitates.

Kersten Then is it not time for you to act independently?

Himmler reacts.

Himmler You know I can't, whilst he's still alive.

Kersten It sounds like he barely is. And he can't be in his right mind or he would have left Berlin by now or made you his successor.

Himmler Yes, but he hasn't.

Kersten So surely you must take matters into your own hands, while there's still time . . . You owe it to your country, don't you?

Himmler looks pained.

Himmler Oh, don't torture me, Kersten. You know I can't betray the Führer. The man to whom I owe everything . . . swore allegiance to him unto death.

He points to his death's head ring.

That's what this ring means. With its skull and crossbones . . . And what of our SS motto? 'My honour is loyalty'.

Kersten Yes, but to whom do you owe that loyalty most? The Führer or the German people?

Himmler I always thought there was no distinction. The Führer was the German people.

Kersten Yes, but now . . . with the country on the point of ruin?

Himmler smiles bitterly.

Himmler It's true. We thought we would take over half of Russia but it is the Russians who are taking over half of Germany . . .

Beat.

But we couldn't have known that the Americans would supply them with the very best weapons . . . Roosevelt said America would be the arsenal of democracy, not of Bolshevism . . . and if it hadn't been for that we'd have beaten them easily, as we did France, Holland and Belgium.

Kersten Perhaps, but it's no use dwelling on the past. You must think of the future and cut your losses.

Himmler Yes, well, I would still like to save a few million more of us from Russian occupation . . . After all, the very biological substance of the German people is now at stake.

Kersten Exactly. So you must make peace with the Western Allies to prevent the Russians going any further. Or even better, to push them back.

Himmler Easy to say, but how?

Kersten By releasing Jews.

Pause.

Himmler Even if that were possible, it wouldn't necessarily bring peace.

Kersten Perhaps not. But they certainly won't make peace with you until you do.

Himmler But I need to keep some as bargaining chips. And to work in the armaments factories, not that we have many left.

Kersten Fine, then keep some. But you must at least get the ball rolling by releasing others.

Himmler considers this.

Himmler How many?

Kersten The more the better, I would say. After all, you have plenty to spare. Certainly those in Ravensbrück, which is so close to Scandinavia they would be relatively easy to transport.

Himmler looks at him.

Himmler I know what you're doing, you know.

Kersten . . . What?

Himmler You were always able to massage a life out of me, weren't you? Or even several lives, as you did with those Swedes we caught spying in Warsaw. Do you remember? They were my Christmas present to you once.

Kersten Of course.

Himmler But not thousands of lives. Now you are overreaching yourself.

Kersten But what is the point in keeping them here?

Himmler We have nothing else. We need to keep something to bargain with.

Kersten So they are hostages . . .

Himmler Yes, if you like.

Kersten But if you give some of them up you will win goodwill and perhaps then the Western Allies will agree to parley with you . . .

Himmler You really think they might, despite all the things they and their press say about me?

Kersten They've had Stalin as an ally these last four years and think what he's done . . . so why not you?

Himmler considers this.

Himmler I see what you mean . . .

He looks at him suspiciously.

Tell me though, why should I listen to you on political matters? Now that Finland's broken away, you're on the Allied side and an enemy of Germany's.

Kersten Only after we lost sixty thousand out of a population of just three and a half million . . . And if we are going to observe the letter of the law, Herr Reichsführer, I should not have given you treatment. As an enemy combatant.

Himmler smiles faintly.

Himmler You're right. Our relationship is above politics . . . and besides, you may have a Finnish passport, but you are an ethnic German, which makes you a German in my book.

Kersten smiles uneasily.

Tell me though, what's in it for you?

Kersten hesitates.

Kersten How do you mean?

Himmler What do you care if the Jews live or die? . . . What difference does it make to you? You don't think any of them will thank you, do you? So why do you exert yourself so much on their behalf?

Kersten I'm a doctor. I care about all human life.

Himmler Even the Jews?

Kersten Yes, even the Jews . . . I am not a National Socialist, remember.

Himmler No, you've always stubbornly refused to join, haven't you? And I wanted to make you an SS general . . .

Kersten I'm too fat to be an SS general.

Himmler Nonsense, look at Goering.

Kersten smiles.

Kersten Goering is an exception.

Himmler Perhaps. But I remember how shocked Ribbentrop was when he found out you weren't even a member of the party. I had to promise that after the war you'd be the first to attend a political training course . . . though I guess you'll be spared that now.

Beat.

So there's no other reason for your wanting to save them?

Kersten No, of course not . . . Why would there be?

Himmler You're not worried about your own position . . . after the war?

Kersten . . . How do you mean?

Himmler As the mass murderer's doctor. The man who relieved the monster's pain, enabling him to do his work.

Kersten . . . Only doing my job.

Himmler Yes, that's what everyone will say . . .

Beat.

But not me. I'm ready to die if necessary.

Kersten For him?

Himmler Yes. And for Germany.

Kersten thinks.

Kersten I remember I once asked you whether you'd kill yourself if Hitler asked you to. And you looked at me, shocked, and said, 'Yes, certainly! At once! For if the Führer orders anything like that, he has his reasons. And it's not for me as an obedient soldier to question those reasons. I only recognise unconditional obedience.' And I said I wouldn't kill myself if the President of Finland ordered me to.

Himmler No, I don't see you as one for self-sacrifice.

Kersten smiles.

Kersten Would you do it now though, if the Führer ordered you to?

Himmler hesitates.

Or kill your wife and daughter? . . . Or Hedwig and the little ones?

Himmler There was a time when I would have done . . . but now . . .

Kersten Well then. Why follow other pointless, or indeed murderous, orders? Like blowing up the camps, and killing the prisoners, as he has ordered you to, rather than allowing them to escape into enemy hands? And in any case, we're only talking about allowing them into the neutral hands of Sweden.

43

Himmler considers this.

Besides, by coming here tonight and meeting a Jew, don't you think you've already made your decision? You've crossed the Rubicon – burned your bridges – and there's no going back.

Himmler But Hitler doesn't know about this.

Kersten And in all probability he won't know about these releases either. Because the man's about to die, isn't he, if he isn't dead already. Either by his own hand or at the hands of the Russians. And by refusing to leave a doomed Berlin, he's effectively given up the leadership, hasn't he? Which leaves you in charge. So it is you who must make the decisions now.

Himmler thinks.

Himmler Perhaps you're right . . . Perhaps there is just no point to it any more . . . We've lost our fight against the Jews – and were always bound to, given that two-thirds of them were out of our grasp in America and elsewhere. And I instinctively recoil from doing anything pointless and irrational. That's where the Führer and I differ. He still hates the Jews above all others and wants to kill as many as possible for its own sake. Take them down with us, as he says . . . But perhaps you're right. Perhaps if we spare the remaining few, we can avoid being ground down so completely and salvage something from the wreckage . . . But maybe that's just an illusion and a fantasy . . .

Kersten Not at all . . . You're absolutely right. Killing Jews is no longer the solution, even in National Socialist terms, but part of the problem.

Himmler Yes, I suppose you could put it like that . . . The Jewish problem has been superseded by the more immediate problem of losing the war. And if releasing some Jews might prevent that, then so be it . . . But unfortunately the Führer doesn't see it that way, and refuses to spare a single one.

Kersten Why hasn't he ordered you to kill them all now then? Why wait for the Allies' approach?

Himmler Because I guess he might release some if the Allies came to him with a good enough peace offer.

Kersten That's not going to happen.

Himmler No . . . and that's why I'm here, I suppose.

Kersten Yes, and that's why I've brought Mr Masur here too . . . So isn't it time you rewarded him for his trouble? So he'll go back to Sweden and the World Jewish Congress singing your praises . . .

Himmler looks up hopefully.

Himmler You really think he might?

Kersten Absolutely. If you release enough prisoners.

Himmler reflects.

So be generous. Expansive. Decent, as befitting an SS man. Show that characteristic Germanic generosity I have so often heard you speak of . . . Be magnanimous.

Himmler thinks.

Himmler Perhaps I could be . . .

Beat.

To the Danish and Norwegian and Dutch prisoners, at least, who are of my own Germanic race after all . . .

Kersten Well . . . yes . . .

Himmler And the French may not be Germanic but are still a great nation with a great history and culture . . .

Kersten Certainly . . .

Himmler But the *Jews* . . . who have sought to destroy us . . .

Kersten Only in self-defence.

Himmler (*firmly*) It was we who were acting in self-defence.

Kersten lets it go.

Kersten . . . You've let Jews go before. From Theresienstadt, for example.

Himmler Yes, and when the Führer found out about it he went berserk and put a stop to it immediately . . . But in any case, I got a good price for them. What would I get this time? Just some vague hopes of goodwill.

He thinks.

No . . . it's not enough . . . I can't do it.

Kersten takes this in.
  Himmler starts getting dressed again and puts on his vest.
  Then his shirt.
  Kersten thinks.

Kersten What about just the women?

Himmler . . . what?

Kersten If you will not let any Jewish men go, allow the Jewish women to . . . What harm have they done you?

Himmler considers this.

And you have always been so chivalrous to women. How often have I heard you say, 'To the Germanic Peoples women are sacred, and sacred is the hearth' . . . And I have never heard an obscene word cross your lips, or anyone else's in your company . . .

Beat.

Himmler Perhaps I could spare the women . . .

Kersten Of course you could.

Himmler Or some of them . . .

Kersten Yes. That would be a noble and humane gesture. As befitting a great German leader and statesman.

Himmler thinks.

Himmler Ask Mr Masur to come back in, please.

Kersten Of course, Herr Reichsführer.

Himmler puts on his jacket.

Himmler And if you don't mind, I'd like speak to him alone for a moment.

Kersten Not at all. Good idea. I shall wait outside.

Himmler Thank you. We shan't be long.

Kersten goes out.
  Himmler does up the buttons of his jacket.
  Then puts his belt on.
  There is a knock at the door.

Come in.

Masur enters as Himmler secures his gun.
  Himmler looks up and sees him.

Ah, Mr Masur. Please come and sit down.

Masur sits.
  Himmler sits opposite him.
  Pause.
  Himmler indicates the remaining pastries.

Would you like a pastry?

Masur No, thank you.

Himmler hesitates.
  Then picks up a pastry and takes a bite out of it.
  He puts the remnants of it back on the plate.
  Masur watches him chew and then swallow.

Himmler Now, I wanted to speak to you alone for a moment because . . . well . . . I want you to know that I personally have never had a problem with your people.

Masur takes this in.

Masur Is that so?

Himmler Yes. It was the Bolsheviks I was against. Though you must admit there was some overlap . . . But that's by the by . . .

Beat.

Look, what I want to say is, as this war has at bottom been a war between your people and mine, it is up to us to end it, is it not?

Masur remembers something.

Masur 'Bury the hatchet'?

Himmler Exactly . . . Now, of course, as you say, not all Jews are Bolsheviks, so why not join hands with us now so we can fight the Russians together?

Masur . . . I'm afraid, Herr Reichsführer, you overrate my power as you have always overrated the power of Jews. But even amongst Jews, I am just a private citizen. So I am not in a position to fight anyone, let alone Russia.

Himmler You are a representative of the World Jewish Congress.

Masur Actually, Mr Storch is, but I am his substitute.

Himmler That is not important, you will be reporting back, will you not?

Masur Of course.

Himmler Well then, isn't it time our two peoples finally made peace before we are all at the mercy of the Bolsheviks?

Masur thinks.

Masur I agree it is time to end the war and free my people, and all the other prisoners.

Himmler And you will pass on what I've said?

Masur Of course.

Himmler Well then. That is all I ask for.

Beat.

As I say, I never wanted to make war with the Jews in the first place. That was Goebbels' obsession. For my part, I've always . . . admired you. Despite our differences. So I'd like to do what I can to help you now . . . though it is not without risk to my own position . . . considerable risk . . .

He looks concerned.

Masur Well, that sounds . . . very decent of you, Herr Reichsführer.

Himmler Good . . . I like to think of myself as decent . . .

He reflects.

And I want you to know that . . . whatever I've had to do in this terrible war . . . I've never acted maliciously . . . but only out of a sense of duty . . . You understand that, I trust?

Masur takes this in.

Masur Oh yes . . . I understand.

Himmler seems satisfied with this.

Himmler Good . . . Then I think we have achieved something . . . rather special tonight . . . Something perhaps unique in the whole war . . . A meeting of minds between a Jew and a National Socialist . . . Who would have thought it possible?

Masur can't help but smile at this.

Indeed, who would even believe this meeting could take place? . . . Though it's to remain a secret, of course.

Masur Of course.

Pause.

Himmler Right, well, now that we understand one another, I think it's time we called Dr Kersten back in to finalise matters, don't you?

Masur As you wish, Herr Reichsführer.

Himmler opens the door.

Himmler Dr Kersten, come back in please.

Kersten Of course, Herr Reichsführer.

Kersten comes back into the room.
  Beat.

Himmler Now, having spoken to Mr Masur, I am now in a position to make him an offer . . . or perhaps I should say gift, as I ask for nothing in return.

Himmler pauses for effect.

So, I am willing to free a thousand Jewish women from the Ravensbrück concentration camp.

This does not get the reaction he was hoping for.
  Masur glances at Kersten.

Masur One thousand?

Himmler Yes . . . That's a nice round number.

Masur It's fewer than you released from Theresienstadt last year.

Himmler Yes . . . but they included men.

He smiles faintly.

The women will, however, be designated as Polish, rather than Jewish . . . I leave you to coordinate their departure with the Swedish Red Cross under Count Bernadotte. But I shall inform him when I see him directly after leaving here of my decision. We are meeting for a six o'clock breakfast at Hohenlychen.

He thinks.

It is crucial, however, that not only your visit here remains secret, but also the arrival of these Jewesses in Sweden.

Masur nods.

Kersten Of course, Herr Reichsführer.

Himmler Otherwise there will certainly be no more releases.

Masur I'll pass that on.

Himmler Do.

Beat.

Masur But what about all the other prisoners you're still holding? Do you promise to keep them safe, and not send them on any more . . . evacuations?

Himmler hesitates.

Himmler I can only say that I will do my best . . .

Beat.

Now, I hope you are satisfied with that, Mr Masur.

Masur Satisfied . . . no. I would like you to release all the prisoners to the Red Cross.

Himmler Yes, well, that is impossible. I've probably been too generous as it is. But in any case, I hope you will accept these thousand Jewesses as a token of my goodwill.

Masur Well . . . I certainly won't refuse them. And it's a start, I suppose.

Himmler Yes, I suppose you could put it like that . . .

Beat.

Masur Would you mind putting it in writing though?

Himmler is taken aback.

So that I have proof of your . . . kind offer, to take back to Stockholm with me.

Himmler thinks.

Himmler Very well. So long as it doesn't get into the press.

Masur It won't.

Himmler takes out a pen as Kersten supplies him with paper. Himmler writes briefly on the desk before handing the paper to Masur.
Masur reads it quickly.

Thank you.

He folds it up and puts it in his pocket.

Himmler Now our task must be to unite Germany and the Western Allies against Bolshevism before it's too late.

Kersten Yes . . .

Himmler Well, goodnight, Mr Masur. Have a safe journey back to Sweden.

Masur Goodnight, Herr Reichsführer.

They look at each other for a moment.
Then Himmler goes out with Kersten.

Himmler Thank you for arranging everything, Dr Kersten. And for the treatment, of course. We can settle up later, I trust.

Kersten Don't mention it. That one was on the house.

Himmler Thank you.

They are now in the hallway.

Kersten Before you go though, I have just one more favour to ask you . . .

Himmler Ah, I should have realised there is no such thing as a free massage.

Kersten It concerns Elisabeth. I have promised to take her to Sweden with me but as she is German I cannot do so without a guarantee of safe passage for her too . . .

Himmler Rats off a sinking ship, eh?

Kersten looks uncomfortable.

Kersten We will, of course, return as soon as it is safe to do so.

Himmler Of course.

Beat.

Very well. I don't wish to part you from your ever-faithful Elisabeth.

He takes a piece of paper out of his pocket and signs it. Then gives it to Kersten.

Kersten Thank you.

Elisabeth comes downstairs in her dressing gown.

Himmler Ah, here she is.

Elisabeth I wanted to see you off, Herr Reichsführer.

Himmler How considerate of you, Miss Lube, even at such a late hour. Or perhaps I should say early hour.

She smiles uncomfortably and looks to Kersten, who smiles back at her.

Speak well of me in Sweden.

Elisabeth sees Kersten smile at her as he holds the document.

Elisabeth Oh, thank you, Herr Reichsführer!

She is close to tears.

Himmler Well, now. I must go to breakfast with Count Bernadotte, who I hope will be able to arrange a meeting for me with General Eisenhower . . .

Kersten Yes . . . of course . . .

Himmler If I could have just one hour with him, I'm sure he will see that I am the only man who can maintain order as we take on the Russians.

Kersten Yes . . .

Himmler looks at Kersten.

Himmler Goodbye then, Dr Kersten.

Kersten Goodbye, Herr Reichsführer.

They shake hands warmly.

And good luck.

Himmler takes this in.
    Then goes.
    The sound of car doors opening and closing, an engine starting and a car driving off.
    Masur joins Kersten and Elisabeth as they watch the car go.

Masur Do you really think Eisenhower will agree to meet him?

Kersten No, poor fool. He's completely deluded. The Western Allies won't touch him with a barge pole. Except to hang him . . . But I wasn't going to tell him that, was I, or why should he bother releasing what he fondly thinks of as his hostages?

The sound of the car fades out.

Come now, it is time for bed. We must try and get some sleep before our journey back to Stockholm.

Kersten turns and walks in.

Elisabeth Yes . . . Oh, Felix, I can't believe I am really going to Sweden to live with you and Irmgard and the children again. It's like a dream.

Kersten Yes, Elisabeth, it is . . . and the nightmare is almost over.

He puts his arm around her and leads her back into the house.
Masur turns to the audience.

Masur It was five o'clock in the morning. Himmler's visit had lasted exactly two and a half hours, and for a short time I had even been alone with him . . . a free Jew face to face with the murderer of millions of my people . . . who seemed to need to defend himself to a Jew . . .

He reflects.

A few hours later, after some intermittent sleep and breakfast, our car arrives and Kersten, Elisabeth and I leave for Berlin . . .

Beat.

We pass refugees heading north, and then, despite Himmler's assurance to me, a column of prisoners, before finally, as the Russian artillery rains down on the city, we at last make it to the airport, only to discover that it is no longer possible to fly direct to Stockholm . . . Kersten gets us on a flight to Copenhagen instead but it seems doubtful if we'll be able to get away. How can a German plane escape the lords of the sky?

Beat.

Suddenly, however, the air becomes 'clean', as the Germans say, and we take off . . . Four hours later, to my great relief, we land safely in Copenhagen, from where we take trains and a ferry back to Stockholm and then head straight to the Foreign Office, where we learn that the Red Cross bus convoy is already on its way to Ravensbrück . . . As we walk out into the evening sunshine, I tell Kersten that Jews all over the world will be eternally grateful to him . . .

A spot comes up on a woman in the striped dress of a concentration camp prisoner, Jeanne Bommezjin.

Jeanne One Sunday afternoon we hear a sudden rumour. The Red Cross is coming to take us away! . . . Those that remain in the camp are half crazed with excitement. But I am past believing rumours. I am much more likely to believe another rumour, namely that they are about to shoot the lot of us now that the camp is surrounded by the advancing allies . . .

Beat.

Then all together and under guard we leave the camp . . .

Beat.

We find ourselves moving in the direction of the gas chambers, and for many of us it is too much. A few are seized with a kind of nervous fit, and we have to calm them, and drag them with us in the column. It is only a few minutes but the tension seems to last for hours . . . Finally, we are safely past the ovens . . . On we go, not daring to think of liberty, for if it does not happen after we have counted on it, we are lost . . . We move on and see the back of the camp – here the stores, there the Siemens factory . . . Women appear behind the windows and the barbed wire to look at us and where we are going, knowing that 'transport' usually means death.

Beat.

And then suddenly pandemonium breaks loose. We scream, weep and cheer as a white bus, flying the Red Cross flag with red crosses on the doors and bonnet, appears round the bend of the road . . . And the people in it smile at us and wave their hands . . . Then more and more buses appear on the road, all marked with the Red Cross . . . The officials ask us if we will mind the long journey, if we'll get nervous or afraid. They don't know that for years we have faced death every moment of the day. Afraid? When our liberty is in sight at last! . . . When we get the order to enter the buses there is a sudden scramble, a fight for a place, because there are not enough buses and no one wants to be left behind. Quite a number have to remain, but the Red Cross officers promise on their word of honour that they will return to collect the remaining prisoners . . . And then we are off . . . As we drive on through the night we hear the explosions of bombs and the rumble of guns, but nothing matters to us other than that we are alive and approaching freedom . . .

Pause.

Masur When Himmler finally realised that he was not destined to lead Germany to a separate peace with the West, he shaved off his moustache, put on the uniform of an ordinary soldier and set out on foot for Bavaria, before being caught at a British command post, where he bit on the cyanide capsule he'd hidden in a tooth he'd had specially drilled for the purpose . . .

Beat.

Dr Kersten, on the other hand, became a Swedish citizen and continued to practise physiotherapy in Stockholm until his death in 1960, when a biography was published entitled *The Man with the Miraculous Hands*.

Pause.

In the end, more than seven thousand women – about half of whom were Jewish – were rescued from Ravensbrück between the 22nd and the 28th of April, 1945 . . . It seems that once the first thousand were released, the dam had been breached and the Red Cross were able to take as many women as were fit to travel . . .

Beat.

It was by far the largest prisoner rescue of the war . . . though to many it felt, as one survivor put it, like just 'a tear in the sea' . . .

He reflects as the lights come up slowly as night passes into dawn.
Blackout.
The End

.